Steps Towards Success

A Practical And Effective Guide To All The Habits Of Successful And Highly Effective People. Overcome Fear, Create A Success Mindset, and Achieve Your Dreams

by
David Cliff Moore

Steps Towards Success

Table of Contents

Introduction

Social anxiety is defined as the deep fear of social situations, specifically unfamiliar ones. Individuals affected by this disorder fear interacting with other people. Just the thought of putting themselves in these situations causes intense anxiety, and so they would do extreme measures to avoid such circumstances.

Symptoms of Social Anxiety:

What are the Symptoms of Social Anxiety?

How can you tell if what you're feeling is not just a simple case of worrying?

Here are some of the common signs of social anxiety?

Excessive worries

Has worrying become a habit for you? If you tend to make a big deal out of everything, even in the smallest things, then you are worrying too much. If the anxiety you're feeling lasts for days and most days of the month that is excessive. If you become so anxious that it interferes with your everyday life, you are probably suffering from anxiety disorder.

If your anxiety results to physical symptoms such as fatigue, there is a high probability you're suffering from the disorder.

Excessive worrying is one of the emotional symptoms of social anxiety.

In addition to too much worrying, you may be suffering from this disorder if you feel any of the following:

-Stressed out from too much worrying

-Feeling and acting foolishly

-Afraid of being negatively evaluated or observed

-Angry and frustrated with yourself

-Panic a lot showing symptoms of panic attacks

-Tired of being so anxious most of the time

-Shameful

-Self-conscious

-Always thinking about embarrassing or humiliating yourself

Irrational and overblown fears

Do you have irrational and overblown fears?

No one is fearless but if you feel overwhelming fear about specific situations like speaking in front of an audience, big or small, it is a definite sign of social phobia. The feeling of fear is paralyzing.

Excessive and irrational fear is one of the telltale signs of social anxiety, and various situations can trigger it. Young people suffering from social anxiety, for instance, are afraid of participating in school activities and performances. They get anxious even asking someone for help. They worry excessively about exercise classes.

In general, situations that involve human interaction can provoke social anxiety including the following:

-Speaking to authority figures

-Speaking in groups

-Getting involved in peer activities

-Meeting people

-Initiating conversations

-Inability to think of anything to say to start or keep a conversation going

-Drinking, eating or signing anything in front of people

-Paying at the counter when shopping

-Inviting people at home

-Being invited to parties

-Going to public restrooms

-Going to school or work

-Having all eyes on you

-Taking exams

-Speaking up in class or in meetings

-Being criticized or teased

Sleeping issues

Do you have trouble sleeping?

Sleep problem is linked to various health conditions. It becomes a sign of anxiety when your sleep troubles happen a lot or on a regular basis. Individuals with social anxiety disorder may find themselves lying awake at night worrying either about a specific issue or nothing particular at all. Do you wake up in the middle of the night feeling wired and cannot seem to calm down? This is only one of the many cognitive and physical symptoms of social anxiety. If you are suffering from this disorder, your excessive fear and worrying may lead to these physical signs:

-Feel faint or lightheaded

-Crying

-Hyperventilation

-Feel an urge to go to the restroom

-Self-criticism

-Uncoordinated and easily distracted

-Stuttering or stumbling over words

-Mind going blank or inability to think straight

-Racing thoughts

-Concentration problems

-Poor short-term memory

Chapter 1:
Dealing With Depression

Cognitive behavioral therapy can help you manage the negative thought process that might be making it difficult for you to overcome depression. Depression keeps you from enjoying the best there is in life.

Constantly thinking about negative things will keep you depressed. According to scientists, people who struggle with depression do not do so for lack of positive thoughts but because they can hardly allow themselves to think about and feel such thoughts.

With depression, the main behavioral change is that people find it difficult to do things, and so they do less and often withdraw from people (Greenberger & Padesky, 2015). The psychological process is referred to as dampening.

Dampening makes you suppress any positive thoughts and emotions. Emotional dampening makes you convince yourself that you do not deserve good things, you do not deserve happiness. Even when something good is happening, you are skeptical, knowing it will not last.

Why does this happen to you when you are depressed? What can you do about it? One possible explanation experts offer is that you give the negative voice in your head a lot of power. It evolves into a pessimistic defense mechanism.

What starts as subtle skepticism manifests into a defeatist thought process because you are afraid of getting your hopes up.

No one wants to play the fool in any situation. In response to this fear, you dampen all positive thoughts to stay safe from disappointment. Unfortunately, disappointment is a part of life. Things will not always go your way.

Understanding Depression

One of the biggest struggles you might be having with depression is a sense of pessimism or negativity. Even when good things are happening, you do not trust that they will remain good for a long time. You worry that it is not real, or it will not last long.

It is okay to open up and feel the things you are feeling. It is only human that you do. However, they should not steal your life from you.

You have a better life ahead of you, and depression cannot take that away from you. There is always a way out. Speak to someone. You best believe it; things do get better.

How Does CBT Help with Depression?

CBT is one of the most successful methods of dealing with depression. It is a gradual process where, with the help of your therapist, you define the behavior patterns you need to change. The idea here is to reach into the part of your brain that suppresses the positive thoughts and recalibrate it to enable you to enjoy the good thoughts.

While CBT is effective, you also have to do so much more on your own outside the therapy sessions. You need to make sure you are in an environment that fosters change instead of making things worse. Start with the people around you.

There should be a concerted effort to help you ignite the positive thoughts in the brain and encourage new patterns. CBT helps to liberate you from negative thought processes.

CBT Techniques for Depression

Following successful studies, most scientists believe individuals who are battling depression barely succeed with self-study. Therefore, you should seek professional help for no less than six weeks.

Your therapist will try to learn more about your case of depression, what makes it worse, and the things you have been through.

There are techniques that your therapist will recommend after understanding what triggers your depression. Here are some possible methods you might work with:

Identifying the Problem

First, your therapist will try to connect with you at a different level and try to get you to let them in. You should try to let them feel the pain you are feeling. Simple conversations with the therapist will help you achieve this milestone.

Where possible, you will be advised to keep a journal. By taking notes, it is easier to refer and make a note of your progress.

Taking notes will also help the therapist identify what is making you depressed. With this figured out, you begin the journey to improving the problem.

A feeling of hopelessness is normal when you are depressed. You feel like things are at their worst and will probably not get any better. You will be advised to write down things that are bothering you, things you are worried about and want to change but, for some reason, you cannot.

Dealing with Negative Thoughts

Since you have already figured out some things that are making you think negatively, the next step would be to counter those thoughts. Note down the negative thoughts that come to mind whenever something happens. These are the thoughts that you give power while suppressing the positive ones.

For each negative thought, you can think of, write a positive statement that you believe can help you overcome it. By writing these thoughts down, they are easier to remember.

Rehearse them and try to speak them to yourself whenever you are caught up in a situation where you cannot think positively.

Rehearsal is a repetitive process that will, in the long run, help you replace negative thoughts with positive thoughts. The brain becomes aware of a new line of thinking and the more you tell yourself these positive thoughts, the easier it will be to replace the negative ones.

Since it might not be easy coming up with the ideal positive thoughts, think about something that is not so far from the negative thoughts. Let's assume the first thing that comes to your mind is: "I am not happy with this life. Things don't seem to be going my way."

An ideal positive thought would be: "People struggle all the time, and my case is no different. I have been through bad times before, and this too shall pass."

Creating New Opportunities

The next step is to discuss ways of encouraging positive thoughts. Even when things are not going according to plan, try to find something positive in a bad situation.

Say you walk into a room but you dislike the furniture arrangement or the window placement. Instead of dwelling on that, you can appreciate the color on the walls or the paintings.

One way of addressing this is to get a friend that can help you manage your excitement.

Evaluate Your Days

At the end of the day, go back to your journal and revisit the events that happened. Visualize the things that made you feel good or you are thankful for.

You can also share some of them online if you wish. By revisiting these thoughts, you are making good progress regarding creating new associations in your mind.

These are new memories that the brain is getting used to and falling in love with. As you keep doing this, you start having a positive outlook and approach to life.

Embrace Disappointment

Things are not always going to go your way. Disappointment is a part of life, and you should accept that. The way you respond to such a situation will determine how fast you can move on.

Your current challenges can be overcome. There is nothing wrong with grieving about a bad situation. It helps you overcome the challenge.

If you have just broken up with someone, it is okay to feel down. However, do not blame yourself for the breakup. Instead, accept that you wanted different things in life and that there is someone out there who will love you just the way you are and in ways no one has ever loved you before.

To embrace disappointment, learn to live within your means. Take each experience you go through as a learning process. Identify your mistakes and promise to correct them in the future. Make changes in your life because they make you feel better and will make you a better version of yourself.

Do not make changes because someone wants you to make them or because it suits the narrative, they wish for you. Negative thoughts might occur from time to time, and this is okay. You should focus

Chapter 2:
Be the Best You

On top of utilizing coping techniques and prescribed treatments, lifestyle changes can significantly help those suffering from mental illness. Lifestyle changes may be seemingly simple, but they are actually very powerful tools when it comes to treating social anxiety. In some people's cases, a lifestyle change is all they may need to recover from anxiety. In the case that a person needs other treatment as well, making good lifestyle changes can help cure anxiety even faster and prevent it from happening again.

Here are a few changes that people can try:

- Exercise: Researchers have found that regularly exercising can be just as effective as medication when it comes to treating depression. Exercises boost the 'feel-good' brain chemicals in the brain, such as serotonin and endorphins. These chemicals also trigger the growth of new brain cells and connections similar to what antidepressants and anti-anxiety medication do.

The best part about exercise is that you don't need to do it intensely in order to have the benefits. Even a simple 30-minute walk can make a huge difference in a person's brain activity. For the best results, people should aim to do 30 – 60 minutes of aerobic activity every day or on most days.

- Social Support: Just like I mentioned earlier, having a strong social network reduces isolation, which is a huge risk factor in anxiety. Make an effort to keep in regular contact with family and friends (ideally on a daily basis) and consider joining a support group or class. You can also opt to do some volunteering where you can get the social support you need while helping others as well.

- Nutrition: Eating properly is important for everyone's mental and physical health. By eating well-balanced and small meals throughout the day, it will help you minimize mood swings and keep energy levels up. Although you may crave sugary foods due to the quick boost that they provide, complex carbohydrates are much more nutritious. They can provide you with an energy boost without a crash at the end.

- Sleep: A person's sleep cycle has strong effects on mood. When a person does not get enough sleep, their symptoms of anxiety may get worse. Sleep deprivation causes other negative symptoms like sadness, fatigue, moodiness, and irritability. Not many people can function well with less than seven hours of sleep per night. A healthy adult should be aiming for 7 – 9 hours of sleep every night.

- Stress reduction: When a person is suffering from too much stress, it exacerbates their anxiety and puts them at a higher risk of developing more serious anxiety disorders. Try to make changes in your life that can help you reduce or manage stress. Identify which aspects of your life creates the most stress, such as unhealthy relationships or work overload and find ways to minimize their impact and the stress it brings.

- Quit smoking: Smoking has been proven to increase anxiety and depression levels due to the mixture of chemicals known to be found within cigarettes. In addition, smoking negatively affects a person's health overall, which can increase feelings of anxiety. Although people with social anxiety may indulge in cigarettes hoping to ease their anxiety, it actually does the opposite.

- Avoid Caffeine and limit alcohol: Avoiding caffeine and alcohol is crucial when it comes to treating anxiety and depression. Caffeine and alcohol are both depressants that tend to cause increased heart rate. Since an increased heart rate is a symptom of anxiety, one can easily confuse the symptoms of caffeine with anxiety and make your overall condition worse.

- Add Omega-3: Omega-3 has been proven to improve brain function and has anti-inflammatory benefits. Research has found that omega-3 has numerous benefits for those who are suffering from mental disorders due to the benefits it brings to a person's brain function. Start by consuming more fish and purchasing high omega-3 eggs rather than regular ones.

Meditation/Relaxation Techniques

Mindfulness is also an element in Cognitive Behavioral Therapy but could be utilized on its own through meditation. So what exactly is mindfulness or meditation? Well, mindfulness is a type of meditation that is used as a mental training practice that requires you to focus your mind on your thoughts and sensations in the present moment. Your thoughts include your physical sensations, passing thoughts, and current emotions.

Mindfulness meditation often utilizes mental imagery, breathing practice, muscle and body relaxation, and awareness of your mind and body. For beginners, it is recommended to follow a guided meditation to direct them through the entire process. If there is nobody guiding you through this meditation, it is easy to drift away and fall asleep. That is not the purpose of meditation. When you become more skilled in doing mindfulness meditation, you will be able to do it without a guide or any vocal guidance.

The most original and standardized program for mindfulness meditation is called the Mindfulness-Based Stress Reduction (MSBR) program.

This meditation was developed by a Ph.D. student who was a student of a famous Buddhist monk. This program focuses on helping the individual bring their awareness to the present and to focus on their own awareness. This meditation has increased in popularity and is not incorporated into medical settings to treat health conditions such as anxiety, insomnia, pain, and stress.

1. Although this meditation is quite straightforward, professionals would recommend you to find a teacher or a program that can act as a guide when you begin. Most people are recommended to do this meditation for at least 10 minutes per day. If you don't have a lot of free time, that's okay. Even just a few minutes a day plays a huge role in changing your wellbeing. Follow these instructions below to get started:

2. Find a place that is quiet, and you feel comfortable in. Ideally, this is your home or a place where you feel safe. Sit in something comfortable like a chair and make sure your head and back are straight and aligned. Try to release any tension you feel.

3. Begin to sort your thoughts and put away the ones that are of the past or future. Focus on your thoughts that are about the present.

4. Begin to bring your awareness to your breath. Focus on the sensation of air moving through your body when you inhale and exhale. Focus on this feeling. Begin to feel the movement of your belly as it rises and falls. Feel how the air enters through your nostrils and leaves through your mouth. Pay attention to how each breath is different.

5. Watch your thoughts come and go in front of you. Pretend you are watching the clouds, letting them slowly pass before you. It doesn't matter if your thought is a worry, anxiety, hope, or fear - when these thoughts pass by, don't ignore them or suppress them. Simply just

acknowledge them calmly and anchor yourself by focusing on your breathing.

6. If you find yourself being carried away by your thoughts, observe where your mind drifted off to, and without judging yourself, simply anchor yourself by focusing on your breathing. This happens a lot with beginners, so don't be hard on yourself if you drift away. Always use your breathing as an anchor.

7. When you are nearing the end of your 10-minute session, sit still for two minutes and bring awareness to your physical location. Get up slowly.

Mindfulness meditation is the simplest technique in the meditation field. However, there are other ways of practicing mindfulness that isn't only in the form of meditation. There are a few opportunities in your day where you can use to practice mindfulness. Here are a few suggestions of when you may have the time to practice mindfulness:

1. Doing the dishes: This is a wonderful window of time where you can use to practice mindfulness. Typically, when you are doing the dishes, there isn't anyone trying to get your attention. This is a perfect time to try mindfulness. Try to focus on the feeling of warm water on your hands, the look, and feeling of bubbles, the smell of your dish soap, and the sounds of your plates clunking in the water. Try to give yourself to this experience and feel your mind refreshing and your anxiety fading.

2. Brushing your teeth: Since you have to brush your teeth every day, you can use this time frame to practice mindfulness. Start by feeling

your weight on your feet against the floor, the feeling of your toothbrush in hand, and the movement as you begin to brush your teeth. Focus on these feelings and the thoughts you are having in the present. Don't dwell; just acknowledge those thoughts as they come and go.

3. Driving: This is one of those activities where it's easy for people to do mindlessly. This is especially relevant if you are driving the same route every day. Make use of this time by not letting your mind wander off to think about tasks that you need to do that day. Practice mindfulness by trying to keep yourself anchored. Take in sensations and visuals like the color of the car in front of you, the smell of your own car, and the feeling of the steering wheel. Focus your attention on all the sounds and noises you hear. If you find yourself wandering, bring your attention back to where you are in your car.

4. Exercising: Make your workout routine a time to also exercise mindfulness. Try to exercise away from screens or music and focus only on your breathing and where your feet are moving. Although watching TV or listening to music will make your workout go by faster or distract you from any anxiety, it won't actually help in managing any unhealthy thoughts. Bring your attention to feeling how your muscles feel and pay attention to how your body is reacting to your workout. Instead of ignoring the pains you may be feeling, acknowledge it, and let yourself feel the exercise.

5. Bedtime: This is normally the time where you begin to get things ready for the next day. Instead of battling too much with it, just keep

in mind what needs to be done. Stop trying to rush through it to get to bed, but try to enjoy the experience of completing those actual tasks. Focus on what needs to be done and don't think about what is next. Start early to leave yourself with enough time, so you don't need to rush through things. Any thoughts or anxieties that come up should be acknowledged and let go.

Help Other People

Helping other people increases one's self-esteem, which produces a positive effect on one's mental health. By helping others, it helps us shift our attention and focus away from ourselves to someone else.

Helping others helps us feel grateful for the things that we have, and it feels good to be able to make a difference for someone using your skills. Focusing on yourself is good, especially when you are trying to grow your self-esteem, but helping other people will help your self-esteem grow as well.

According to scientific research, when people help others, the portion of their brain that is responsible for joyful and rewarding feelings becomes activated. That area of the brain that is activated releases the hormones that make us feel good.

What are some ways that you could help others? The simplest and most straightforward way is to just start volunteering in your community. It could be working with children, the homeless, or even just at your local library. This is a good way of gaining some perspective of people that are less fortunate. Often times, some of the things that people are upset with not having, or the constant comparing to others, is immediately gone when you spend some time experiencing how less fortunate people get by.

Certain things that people used to be upset about becomes trivial when they gain a new perspective. Here are a few questions to consider when it comes to helping others:

- Do I like being around children, the elderly, or animals?
- How much of my time am I able to offer to others?
- What belongings do I have and no longer need that someone else can benefit from having?
- What skills do I have that local non-profits in my city could use?
- Do I have the financial resources to donate to a nonprofit of my choice?
- What am I generally interested in?

The way you help others doesn't have to be a grand gesture. You can do something very simple, like paying it forward. You can simply leave behind a few dollars for the next person at your local drive-thru or coffee shop.

This will make the day for the next person in line. Or you can just take a friend or family member out for dinner for no reason. There are so many little nice things that you can do for others that will help increase your self-esteem.

Find a Sense of Purpose

Finding a sense of purpose can help improve a person's overall mental state. Without purpose, you begin to stop living your life, and you are 'surviving' it instead. Goals help us stay focused and motivated and creates something for people to work towards and look forward to. Begin simply by thinking about what you care about; this could be your family, your pets, or your career. Identify what it is that you are most passionate about in your life and derive your goals from there.

For instance, if you are passionate about animals, you may want to set a goal of starting your own animal shelter or conservatory. It can even be a much smaller goal, like volunteering at the humane society every week. Whatever it is, choosing a goal for yourself helps create a sense of purpose that will motivate you to stay healthy and focused in your life.

Consider Following a Spiritual Path

Following a spiritual path is a method that people have used to manage their mental health. Meditations such as Zen meditation is meant to help uncover a person's innate clarity and workability of the mind. Different from the basic forms of meditation, Zen meditation tackles deep-rooted issues and general life questions that often lack answers.

Zen meditation delves deeper than other meditation techniques that focus on relaxation and stress relief. Zen meditation is described as "A special transmission outside the teachings; not established upon words and letters; directly pointing to the human heart-mind; seeing nature and becoming a Buddha" by the famous Buddhist master Bodhidharma.

Zen meditation is often learned and practiced in schools of Zen. They normally practice the sitting meditation called zazen. It begins with sitting upright and following the breath, with an emphasis on the movement within the belly. Traditionally, the practice requires a deep and supportive connection between teacher and pupil. In this case, it would be a Zen master and a dedicated student.

Rather than creating or offering temporary solutions to day to day life problems, Zen meditation aims to address core issues. It explores the true causes of unhappiness and dissatisfaction and redirects our focus in a way that brings about true understanding. In this theory, the true key to happiness and well-being isn't wealth or fame. In fact, the key lies within all of us.

Chapter 3:
Why Overthinking?

Letting negativity build up in your life for a long time can bring a lot of consequences. Thankfully, we have found a way of overcoming and eliminating negativity. After overcoming and eliminating negativity, you have to deal with any consequences that may be left behind.

It is easy to eliminate someone or a bad habit but the consequences caused by that habit may stay around much longer. For instance, you may decide to eliminate your behavior of sexual promiscuity after a long time.

While it is a positive step in your life, the consequences associated with such behavior such as STIs may remain behind. The same case applies to negativity and negative emotions. You may finally find a way of eliminating negative energy but the consequences of negativity may remain behind.

One of the biggest consequences of negativity is overthinking. You may find that people who have suffered abuse or failure end up overthinking. Overthinking is mainly caused by negativity. The feelings of failure, unworthiness, and remorse often lead to overthinking.

Different Causes of Overthinking

There are many causes of overthinking associated with negativity. Although some people overthink in a positive way, many people overthink negatively. Some of the negative causes of overthinking include:

Low self-esteem: When a person is suffering from low self-esteem, they will often be found in isolation and deep thoughts. Suffering from low self-esteem is a consequence of letting negativity take root to the core. When you allow negative poisonous words of people get into your system, you start believing that you are worthless. Low self-esteem brings constant feelings of undeserving. Some individuals suffering from low self-esteem may contemplate suicide and often suffer from anxiety.

Fear: Another cause of overthinking is fear. Fear is brought about by thinking of the future and the past. If a person is not sure where life is headed, they will be found thinking a lot. A person who is afraid of something will keep on thinking about it. Fear causes someone to have subconscious thoughts about something. Even if you are not thinking about it actively, you will often find your subconscious mind drifting back to that instance. The best way to overcome this type of overthinking is facing your fear. Once you deal with the situation that is giving you so much fear, you will forget about it and live your life in happiness.

Shame: Shame causes overthinking to most people, even those who are emotionally strong. If you go through a shameful instance, it might be public humiliation or something that happened in a closed group you feel embarrassed. In either case, being exposed to public ridicule or being ashamed in front of family members may lead to overthinking. Although it is normal for a person to think about a shameful moment, letting your mind be focused on shameful moment's builds negativity.

If you choose to focus on moments of weakness you take away your ability to focus on the future. Shame is something that will always be part of life. You must remind yourself that the shameful instance only occurred once and that it is not likely to happen. If you come to a place where you can encourage yourself to rise above shame, you build your self-esteem and build positivity. The best way to overcome shame and negativity is to always remind yourself that shameful moments don't last forever. A shameful moment may just last for a few days but it will eventually go away.

Steps Towards Success

Chapter 4:
What Are The Symptoms Of Overthinking?

Overthinking is a disorder that must be corrected. If it is not handled early enough, overthinking may develop into other mental disorders that are more painful and costly. Here are the top symptoms of overthinking.

- You relive embarrassing moments in your head:

If you find yourself constantly living in an embarrassing moment, you are probably suffering from overthinking. It is okay to think about embarrassing moments but you should not relive the moment constantly. When you relive a moment, you feel like that moment is happening again right in your head. You may even show facial expressions of embarrassment. If people around you start asking why you act embarrassed, chances are that you are behaving embarrassed.

- Trouble going to sleep

The most obvious sign of overthinking is sleeping problems. People who overthink find it hard shutting the brain down. You may find yourself straining your brain to settle but nothing works. If you realize that you stay up late and wake up early, you need to examine your thinking process. You may be paying too much attention to the past or the future.

- You ask yourself a lot of questions

Do you find yourself asking what-if questions? If you ever spend your time thinking about what would have happened if you had done things the other way, you are suffering from overthinking. "What if" questions will never add anything to your life. Spending too much time wondering if you would have done things right does not make things right.

Even if you make the biggest mistake of your life, you must accept that it has already happened and move on to the next phase. Spending too much time wondering what would have happened if you would have done things differently does not make things different. It only makes it hard for you to go past that specific moment.

- You try to find hidden meaning in people's words

Overthinking often leads to paranoia. You will find yourself looking at everybody with a third eye. You start looking for hidden meanings in what people say. Overthinking especially in relationships is associated with insecurity. You are unable to trust the person around you and you constantly ask investigative questions. You often find yourself drawing conclusions based on someone's words. Most people who overthink often end up starting rumors or conspiracy theories. You start imagining that there are things that happen in this world that you do not know about.

- Going over past conversations in your mind

Do you find yourself trying to redo an interview or a conversation you had before? People who overthink tend to focus on past conversations. They try making the conversation better in their mind and sometimes may be heard speaking out loud. One of the main symptoms of overthinking is speaking to yourself. Your thinking gets too loud to an extent that it cannot be contained in the mind.

You relive conversations to the extent of speaking them out as if you were having the same conversation again. In most cases, people overthink when a conversation did not go right. Probably, you answered an interview question in the wrong way. Unfortunately, overthinking or rehashing a conversation does not make anything better. When you get such thoughts coming back to your mind, you must dismiss them. Being self-aware of your thought process will help you stop overthinking.

- Lack of concentration

People who overthink are often found lost in another world. If you are constantly found lost in your thoughts and unaware of what is happening around you, you are probably overthinking. When you overthink, your mind is transported to another world. You do not pay attention to what you are doing and in most cases; you may run into an accident. If you realize that people often have to tap your shoulder for attention or call your name out a loud, you have to start examining your thinking process. At this stage, your thought process has been corrupted to such an extent that you no longer live in the real world. Most of your days are spent in another world reliving moments from the past

- You are always worried

Worries are as a result of overthinking. When a person overthinks, he/she keeps on wondering what if this and that may happen. These thoughts may focus on the future or the past. When a person is thinking about the past, he/she will worry about the consequences of the choices they made in the past. You will find yourself asking questions like; what if I was wrong? On the other hand, people may also think about the future. What if such things happen in the future?

Thinking about the future and the past will only give you unnecessary worries. Things that have already happened cannot be redone. The future is something abstract. Until you understand that the future only exists in your mind, you will keep on wasting a lot of time thinking about tomorrow. You should always remind yourself that life is good today and that you should enjoy it.

How To Control Overthinking

You need to find a way of controlling your thoughts. Controlling your thoughts is not easy especially after going through an embarrassing moment. However, you need to control your thinking for your own good. There are many ways to control your thinking.

Be aware of your thoughts: Try practicing self-awareness if you find yourself constantly drifting to another world. When you are aware of your thoughts, you will interrupt them and stop thinking in the same direction. Unfortunately, most people who suffer from overthinking disorder do not even recognize that they are overthinking. When a person is in a state of thinking, the thoughts keep on piling up in a chain process, with one leading to another.

To enhance your awareness, start practicing self-awareness in your daily life. A practical exercise includes reflecting on your thought process after every few minutes. Ask yourself what you have been thinking about the last 1 hour or 30 minutes. You may even set reminders on your phone to help you check your thought process after a few minutes. The reminder will constantly get you out of your negative thoughts and set you on the right path again. Self-awareness should help you forgo thinking and start focusing on your life at the moment.

- Choose the things you want to think about

If you realize that overthinking is always occupying your mind, find something different to think about. This will help you deal with the negative thoughts that go through your head. You may decide to think about the most beautiful things in your life. If you have someone you love, you may choose to think about their beauty and everything good they add to your life. Finding a different focal point for your thoughts will help you control your thought process.

In essence, the two basic ways of controlling your thinking are interrupting your thought process and focusing on a different thinking direction.

Since overthinking is about negativity in most cases, you need to interrupt the continuous flow of negative thoughts in your head. Stop any thought that does not lead to productivity through self-awareness and setting reminders.

This will prohibit you from going deep into the world of negativity. Once you interrupt the thought process from negativity, focus it on beauty. Look at your life and think about things that are beautiful, lovely and attractive. Life has both positive and negative sides. Although the mind always wants to focus on simple mistakes and negative events, you are the one to control the negativity.

You may train your mind to start thinking positively and concentrate on positivity at all times. Once you can stop your thoughts and redirect them, you completely gain control over your thinking and as a result, manage to control overthinking.

How To Stop Overthinking

It is one thing to control overthinking but a different story entirely to stop it. Controlling overthinking entails interrupting and disrupting the overthinking process. You may use reminders and other thoughts to interrupt your mind and control overthinking.

However, most often than not, people who try disrupting the thinking process without addressing the root cause often drift back into their thoughts. To stop overthinking, you need to address the cause from the root. You need to examine the cause of your thoughts and deal with it. Controlling overthinking only deals with the symptoms, but stopping overthinking deals with the root cause.

Here is a simple step by step process to help you stop overthinking.

Step 1: Find the root cause: The first thing you need to do is find the root of your thinking. As soon as you notice that there are symptoms of overthinking showing up in your life, examine your thought process to determine what you are constantly thinking about. In most cases, you will find that you think because of worry or fear.

If you are afraid or worried about something happening, you will spend a lot of time thinking. The positive side of overthinking is usually due to anticipation. Even anticipation of good things should not occupy your mind. You must deal with all these factors to totally stop overthinking about things that may or may not happen.

Step 2: Accept the situation: You need to accept the situation that has led to your fears and worries. You need to accept that this has already happened and that there is nothing you can do about it. However, if there is something you can do about it to make it better, take action immediately. Taking action to stop something bad from happening will also alleviate thinking. Constantly thinking about something that already happened or is about to happen does not help. If it is something that has already happened, except that it is done. If it something that is yet to happen, you can take action about it. Taking action does not necessarily mean stopping it from happening but reducing consequences if possible. Think about your worries and examine the ones you can salvage. If there is nothing you can salvage, stop thinking about it and take action.

Step 3: Face your fears and address your worries: Overthinking is null thinking process that does not result in any solution. However, you need to stand up to your fears if you want to stop thinking about it. The first thing you should do after examining the cause of your worries is to ask yourself what you can do about it. In the case of fear, you only have an option of facing it. Facing your fears entails preparing yourself to stand for your rights and being ready for the consequences of your mistakes. Some of the ways to face your fears include accepting punishment, offering an apology, grieving in terms of loss among others. If you have been overthinking because of a mistake you did at the office, you may choose to face the fear by offering an apology and being ready to take the consequences. One of the things you must constantly keep in your mind is that life cannot be determined by one instance. Even when you lose a job, always remember that there is another option for you. You should be ready to face the consequences of every situation knowing that it's just a moment in life. That moment does not stop life from moving on any grounds.

Step 4: Move on: The other big cause of fear is staying in the past. Whatever happened has already happened and thinking about it does not take it away. In fact, spending too much time thinking about it only brings pain. People who have been heartbroken in relationships tend to spend too much time thinking about the past.

You must find a way of dealing with such thoughts. The thoughts of having a relationship with a person who has already rejected you only bring pain. To completely stop the overthinking process, move on.

Moving on means that you open a new chapter in life. If you are overthinking because you lost a job, open a new chapter by starting a business or looking for another job. If it is due to a broken relationship, move on to another relationship. If it is due to the loss of life of a friend, accept the realities and move on.

Chapter 5:
Procrastination

What Causes Procrastination?

I f procrastination is something that everyone has to deal with at multiple points throughout their life, can it really be all that bad? Despite the many health and well-being risks associated with habitual procrastinating and overthinking, there are still those who refuse to believe that their personal habits and compulsions are under control and far from being dangerous to their mind or body.

Pro Tip: This denial is one of the challenges all people wanting to take control of their habits and behaviors must overcome before any forward progress can be made.

If someone is unwilling to acknowledge their issue and make a conscious decision to change, then they are not going to be able to improve their behaviors or psychological habits.

However, there is plenty of hope and proven techniques out there that have made all the difference for those wanting to give up procrastinating and overthinking.

The most recent studies have shown that the development of habitual procrastination can be traced back to four main psychological causes:

Unable to Focus or Gain Control of Thoughts: Sometimes people who have difficulty with controlling their thoughts or getting themselves to focus have their behaviors being controlled by their emotions rather than their logical thoughts. Emotions are truthful and powerful, but they are also unpredictable and capable of changing without warning, especially for those with existing psychological conditions.

Fear of Failure & Fear of the Unknown: These are perfectly natural phobias that every person faces at some point in their life. While for many the fear disappears once a plan has been made or more information has been gathered, but for others these types of fears (which can be encountered in nearly any given situation) can lead to full-blown panic attacks and other emotional reactions can affect their behavior and inspire psychological habits like procrastination and overthinking to take control of all thought and action.

Lack of Motivation & Low Levels of Energy: These two traits are often connected as many who find themselves trying to cope with procrastination also have experience with larger psychological concerns like depressive states, suicidal behaviors in extreme cases, and the development of anti-social behaviors related to lack of confidence or faith in their own talents, abilities or future potential. This negative thinking constantly circling through their mind can leave damage on an individual's self-esteem, a negative emotion that comes with physical side effects such as fatigue, low immune system efficiency and muscle soreness throughout the body with little to no physical strain to cause it.

Need to Reach Perfection: This is a common trait that comes with the fear of failure and is one of the main causes of procrastination. Through their previous experiences with procrastination and their tendency to overthink, they begin to believe that the only way they will be able to complete something or come to a proper resolution is if their application is totally flawless. Of course, perfection is an often impossible bar for people to reach, particularly when distractions, interruptions and unwelcome challenges can arise at any time and throw off even the most well-planned solutions.

There are still those out there that argue habits like procrastination and overthink cannot be nearly as harmful as people claim they are since everyone deals with them at some point but not everyone falls prey to their control of behaviors and reactions to situations throughout life. Recent studies have looked into this fact as well as determined that the reason not everyone develops dangerous psychological habits because there are those in the population that are more susceptible to the negative and long-term effects than others.

In the following comical chart, it is easy to see the type of distracting thoughts and actions people take when avoiding their tasks and responsibilities, along with the fluctuations in stress levels that come with giving in to habitual procrastination.

While the image itself may have a comical tone, it is an accurate and widely relatable visual of the types of thoughts that dominate someone's mind when procrastination habits have control over a person's mind, emotions and behaviors.

What Kinds of People Are Most Likely to Become Procrastinators?

Like with all psychological habits and behaviors there are some with different personalities and lifestyle variables that can be more or less likely to develop procrastination or overthinking habits. Some of these common variables and personality types include:

Perfectionists: People who struggle with being a perfectionist often also have difficulties controlling their impulse to procrastinate. One of the main reasons for this is because people who take pride in perfection and faultless execution in everything they do are less concerned with not getting a task done than they are finishing something that is flawed in any form. However, for many procrastinating perfectionists, the closer their deadline comes or the higher the pressure gets for them to take action, the more panic sets in an they find themselves in a panicked frenzy to complete their task.

Students: Students, regardless of age or education level, are some of the most common victims of procrastination and overthinking. One of the reasons for this is often connected to a lack of confidence in their own talents and abilities that causes them to obsess about each and every detail of their assignments until they are trapped in a whirlwind of thoughts that keeps them from completing their task.

Another one of the main reasons for student procrastination is the self-deception that comes with the belief that they perform better under the pressure of a nearly impossible deadline.

Despite being told over and over by their friends and family that they will not only feel better, but that the quality of their work will improve if they didn't procrastinate, the impulse is too strong in many cases and the need to put off their responsibilities takes over.

Pro Tip: Those who use this excuse are able to convince themselves that they will be able to complete their task to their best ability even in the shortened amount of time typically because they have done it before. It only takes one successful event for the habit to start and take control.

The first time someone procrastinates and is still able to complete their task or find their solution in time for someone to start procrastinating as a matter of habit and compulsion.

People Pleasers: Those who find themselves constantly surrounded or often outnumbered by people who are difficult to please often become procrastinators. These types of people are eager for those around them (both peers and superiors) to see them in a certain light.

It could be that they lied or fictionalized something about themselves in order to paint this picture for their friends or co-workers, or it could be that there is no reason for the person to feel inferior to those around them because they are just as experienced or talented, but do not see it because their self-esteem has been so wrecked by their procrastinating and overthinking habits.

Those Who Have Learned Through Experience: Those who procrastinated until they were under the gun and managed to come out on top without consequence once or twice by accident are more likely to develop a problem with habitual procrastination because their experience has taught them that they are still able to put out quality work or make solid decisions without having to spend the effort and energy on the time management skills and patience it would take to achieve their goal in a timely and comparatively stress-free manner.

While they may consider themselves lucky at first, the longer this habit is allowed to develop and is practiced by the individual, the further the quality of their work and performance (often in various aspects of their life) will slip until those they work or interact with take notice and action.

The Connection Between Procrastination & Overthinking

While the two are often symptoms of a larger psychological concern that should be acknowledged and explored, habitual procrastinating and overthinking have also been linking as being the cause for one another. Overthinkers who consider themselves driven and motivated in everything they do find that over time, their psychological habit of obsessing over small interactions or replaying regrets through their mind can develop into habitual procrastination over time as these individuals try to find ways to distract themselves from their dominating thoughts and emotions, often pushing aside responsibilities or pressing tasks to avoid having to think about them.

Alternately, those who start as procrastinators may find over time that they are overthinking more and more about the things happening around them, personally and professionally. One of the main reasons for this is that those who are self-aware enough to recognize their impulse to procrastinate in matters from choosing where they want to eat dinner to delivering a major presentation to their employers are also emotionally intelligent enough to realize that the anxiety and panicked emotions that come with that habit are only increasing their stress and decreasing their chances of success. Unfortunately, although they are aware of their habitual procrastinating and overthinking, the compulsive behaviors associated with those habits are more powerful than rational thinking and are often determined by how the individual is feeling at any given moment. This only makes the habitual overthinking worse as it brings up questions like why the person can't just make themselves take an action or make a decision and why they start procrastinating every time they face something, knowing how much stress, regret and guilt comes with the process.

Another connection that is common between the development of procrastination and overthinking habits is a third psychological stage that is fueled by emotions like the fear of failing and the awareness of passing time and burning energy that could be used more productively. This stage is an overwhelming guilt that also comes with negative health and wellness effects like fluctuating stress levels and uncertainty of one's ability to accomplish anything.

Use This Newly Gained Knowledge & Get the Answers You Have Been Searching For!

Now that the knowledge has been collected, it is time to put it to use and start preparing for those first steps forward with taking control of your mind, behaviors and emotions in order to conquer your habitual overthinking and/or procrastination.

As with any plan, the first step is to take a step back and analyze the situation as a whole. Answer these questions about yourself or the person you are concerned for to get a better read on the big picture and the individual factors that may affect treatment:

What behaviors have you noticed that could be connected to habitual procrastination or overthinking?

What is the individual's personality type? Do they fall into the category of higher risk personalities?

What specific factors could be causing the habitual procrastination or overthinking?

Are there certain situations where their behaviors, thoughts and actions (or lack thereof) can be identified as compulsive or driven by emotion rather than rational decisions?

Have you (or the individual in question) acknowledged and accepted that there is a problem with these habitual compulsions that is hindering their ability to function at their full potential?

Chapter 6:
Mindfulness

Learning how to practice mindfulness is very important. It can help you to be more aware of yourself and your surroundings. It can really help you to understand your emotions.

You can figure out what you are feeling, why you are feeling that way, and how you should respond to those feelings. If you are feeling down, practicing mindfulness can bring you back and help you to find positivity when you need it the most.

Being mindful can teach you to pay attention to the smaller details and really live in the moment. It will allow you to live life to the fullest and appreciate everything that life has to offer.

Understanding mindfulness can benefit you by showing you how you may benefit by practicing mindfulness and allowing yourself to become more mindful. Learning to practice mindfulness will teach you how to become a master of your own mind and develop a sense of awareness of both yourself and the world outside of yourself. You may incorporate mindfulness into your life by a few simple and quick habits.

It's easy to make your daily routine more mindful and to check in with yourself occasionally and be more mindful of your thoughts, actions, and emotions. To stay motivated on your mindfulness journey, you must recognize and remind yourself of the benefits of mindfulness. You may not have even heard of mindfulness, but it is a great tool to incorporate into your life to make the most of your everyday life.

What is Mindfulness?

To practice mindfulness, you must know what it is and how you can practice it. It is more than simply thinking or having a mind. Mindfulness is the tool that you can use to be fully aware of yourself and your surroundings.

It means that you are present in the moment instead of being distracted by the outside world, the past, or the future. Instead of worrying, you will be fully focused on the present. When you are mindful, you will be able to concentrate on what is currently happening. You may realize what it is that you are doing and how that makes you feel.

It is so tempting to get caught up in a number of distractions. Our devices constantly have new notifications on them. There is always a new person to talk to, a new task to complete, or a new place to visit. We get caught up in the shows we watch, the games we play, and everything happening around us.

However, it's important to not lose touch with reality. Sometimes, it's crucial to bring your focus back to yourself and really concentrate on what's going on. Instead of worrying about the future or regretting the past, you must be able to concentrate on the present moment. If you are always waiting for happiness, it will never come. You must be able to live in and enjoy the present moment so that you can really live your life instead of having it always control you.

Mindfulness is also about not being completely reactive to everything. Sometimes, it's necessary for you to just live in the moment instead of reacting to it.

Instead of being overwhelmed by everything happening, you can learn to enjoy all of the details. Instead of letting your judgment rule you, you can go with the flow and just live. It can allow you to be more curious about the world around you instead of making immediate assumptions and letting your first thoughts influence your behavior. You will allow yourself to think more deeply and truly reflect on what is going on.

Mindfulness is a natural quality; it is instinctual to be mindful. One doesn't create mindfulness. It is, rather, a skill that must be sharpened and looked into.

You must learn how to access your mindfulness and use it the best that you can. Much like building your biceps with arm exercises, you can strengthen your mindfulness with practice and certain techniques.

You don't need to change yourself to develop mindfulness. You only need to bring out the best of yourself to use it well. Anyone can learn how to be more mindful. It is a way of living, and you can make it a part of your routine. It is easy to learn, and it has been proven to provide you with results. When you are mindful, you will be able to accept what is going on around you without adding your own judgment to it. It is a way of existing and appreciating what is happening.

Practicing Mindfulness

To build a habit, you must learn how to practice it. This is true for mindfulness. You must learn how to practice mindfulness so that you can begin practicing it in your life. Once you understand how to practice mindfulness, you can begin incorporating it into your life and make it a part of your routine

It can help you to improve your day and become more aware of your surroundings. With practice, mindfulness can come naturally to you. Although it will take effort at first, mindfulness can be a very simple habit to incorporate into your life.

To practice mindfulness, you will have to become more aware of your thoughts. Instead of allowing yourself to become absorbed in your worries, reacting to the world around you, or adding your judgment to each situation, you must become focused on the present and your life.

It's important to develop a connection to the world around you and to be able to pay attention to how you feel and think. Mindfulness is about learning how to center your focus back to yourself instead of allowing yourself to get caught up in all of these thoughts.

You can practice mindfulness anywhere. You may choose to practice mindfulness during a routine activity, such as taking a shower or eating breakfast. Mindfulness is appropriate for any time, any place, and any person. You can choose to practice mindfulness while in motion or while staying still. What's important to remember is that you must be able to focus and shut off all distractions.

When practicing mindfulness, you will instead focus on yourself and the world around you. It is as simple as paying attention to your senses. Focusing on your movement, breathing, anything that you smell, and more can make a huge difference.

You are always going to smell, taste, hear, see, and feel. However, you aren't aware of your senses when you are lost in thought. It takes focus to be able to experience those senses.

When you become mindful, you are more aware of what those senses are experiencing. You are tapping into what is already there but typically ignored.

Mindfulness also involves an awareness of your thoughts. You constantly have new thoughts, process them, judge them, and generate more thoughts from them.

However, mindfulness involves observing your thoughts. Instead of processing them and judging them, you can listen to your thoughts. Just allow them to happen without feeling the need to do anything with them.

Thoughts are constantly changing. Allow yourself to observe your thoughts moving from one subject to another without feeling the need to dive deeper and act on those thoughts.

When you let your thoughts take over you, you will become overwhelmed, stressed, and anxious. By allowing yourself to be higher than those thoughts, you are separating yourself from your thoughts.

You can be present in the moment instead of getting caught up in a path to the past or future. You will feel much better knowing that you have the power to control your thoughts, not let them control you.

Incorporating Mindfulness

Incorporating mindfulness into your life is easier than you would think. There are many ways that you can incorporate it into your life, as it is very versatile.

Mindfulness can be practiced at home, at work, and even while you're out. It doesn't take any special tools or supplies to practice mindfulness, and it doesn't cost any money. While there are ways that you can add to your experience, such as getting a mindful meditation app or taking a class to become more mindful, you can practice mindfulness yourself whenever and wherever you would like. You may even pair it with activities that you already do every day.

One way that you may incorporate mindfulness into your life is by practicing it during every meal. Instead of mindlessly eating while going on your phone or watching the television, eat with mindfulness. Really take the time to focus on your food and eliminate other distractions.

Not only will you feel more satisfied, but you will feel fuller and more nourished, which can eliminate the habit of overeating. You will never "miss" a meal, as you will be focused on your food. Take the time to enjoy every bite. Pay attention to how your food looks, tastes, and smells. This will help you to live in the present and enjoy your mealtime much more.

Start practicing mindfulness in every aspect of your routine. When you shower, enjoy the feeling of the water hitting your skin, really massage the shampoo into your scalp and relish in its refreshing, clean feeling. While driving, focus on the road; practice mindfulness instead of letting your mind wander.

Choose activities that you can really put your focus on. Pick a hobby that you feel passionately about. It's great to have something that you can fully invest yourself into and distract yourself from your thoughts with. You may like reading and getting lost in a good book. Perhaps running is your way of focusing.

No matter what it is, having a hobby that you really enjoy and can focus on is great. You may also want to try new things, as you can get lost in the thrill of newness. Travel somewhere new, try new foods, switch your routine around, or decorate your house. You will find that you are more mindful in the present when you experience new experiences.

Chapter 7:
Resilience and Stoicism

Everyone has not welcomed the renewed popularity of Stoicism. Stoicism is sometimes criticized as an outdated philosophy, a relic of ancient thinking with no place in the modern world.

Some people say it's unrealistic, that we can't really control our emotions just by changing our belief system. Other people say we shouldn't even try and that Stoicism would keep us from ever experiencing love or joy. Does Stoicism increase good feelings as its practitioners' claim, or does the rejection of the passions lead to a gray life with no emotional depth?

The great Stoics, like Epictetus, taught that our thoughts are the main source of our happiness and unhappiness in life. So, how well does Stoicism match up with what we know about the brain? If Stoic ideas have any validity, they should be confirmed by modern psychology and cognitive science.

There are many different therapies in the practice of psychology, including everything from traditional Freudian psychotherapy to acceptance and commitment therapy.

One of the most effective and widely used treatments is known as Cognitive Behavioral Therapy or CBT.

CBT is used in the treatment of anxiety, mood disorders, eating disorders, depression, gambling addiction, substance abuse, and many other common problems. Studies have shown it to be one of the most effective and practical types of therapy, and it is considered the preferred treatment for a wide range of cognitive and behavioral issues. Studies have shown it to be just as effective as medication in some cases, making it the ideal option for people who want to address their problems without medication if possible.

Although CBT is a treatment method rather than a philosophy, the core ideas of this therapy are based on ancient Stoicism. Practicing Stoicism is not the same thing as receiving treatment in Cognitive Behavioral Therapy from a qualified professional, and receiving CBT treatment won't make you a philosopher. The two are distinct. Nevertheless, the tools CBT therapists use are based on the insights of Epictetus, Seneca, and Marcus Aurelius—a powerful argument for the validity of the Stoic worldview.

Cognitive Behavioral Therapy is a broad term, encompassing several different methods. Cognitive Emotional Behavioral Therapy, Structured Cognitive Behavioral Training, Moral Recognition Therapy, Stress Inoculation Training, Unified Protocol, Mindfulness-based Cognitive Behavioral Hypnotherapy, and Brief Cognitive Behavioral Therapy are all types of CBT.

All these therapies have slightly different theories and techniques, and some incorporate other influences along with Stoicism. For instance, Mindfulness-based Cognitive Behavioral Hypnotherapy incorporates some ideas from Buddhism. However, the basic insights and assumptions of CBT are shared by all the variations, and all of them share the same roots in ancient Stoicism.

Development of CBT

Cognitive Therapy was developed in the 1960s by a psychoanalyst named Aaron Beck, who felt that traditional psychotherapy was too focused on the unconscious to be practical for most patients.

Beck's reading of the Stoics had convinced him that psychological problems are often influenced by how people think and what they believe about the world. This matches several passages in the Meditations of Marcus Aurelius, where the emperor reminds himself that our beliefs and opinions are the prime cause of all our actions.

According to Beck, negative feelings and behaviors are often the direct consequence of negative beliefs and thoughts. He wanted to help patients recognize distorted thought patterns so that they could transform them over time into more positive and functional thought patterns. Beck believed that this would naturally lead to a decrease in dysfunctional behaviors, making Cognitive Therapy an effective treatment for substance abuse and other behavioral problems.

Cognitive Therapy is based on Beck's Cognitive Model, which divides human thought into three categories: automatic thoughts, intermediate beliefs, and core beliefs. Automatic thoughts are involuntary negative reactions based on the patient's underlying beliefs about the self, other people, or the future.

For example, a person suffering from an eating disorder might have a feeling of revulsion and self-hatred when looking in a mirror, imagining herself to be much heavier than she really is. Automatic thoughts derive from intermediate beliefs in an "if-then" pattern, for example, "if I lose enough weight, I'll finally be popular." Intermediate beliefs derive from core beliefs such as, "nobody likes me." By tracing the automatic thought all the way back to the core belief that ultimately inspired it, it becomes clear that this patient's eating disorder is based in a deep belief that she is unlikeable and that treating this belief is key to treating the behavior.

In Cognitive Therapy, the therapist helps the patient learn to recognize automatic thoughts, then identifies the intermediate and core beliefs driving automatic thoughts. By asking a series of questions (a method borrowed from Socrates), the therapist demonstrates the irrational nature of these beliefs. Finally, the therapist helps the patient understand that these beliefs and automatic thoughts are distorted and inaccurate.

This process mirrors the Stoic approach to cognition, in which automatic reactions or "impressions" are subjected to questioning and only "assented to" if they seem rational by Stoic standards. Essentially, the Cognitive Therapist teaches the patient to question his impressions and assent only to those who turn out to be rational after close examination. Epictetus would certainly approve.

Cognitive Behavioral Therapy takes the basic idea of Cognitive Therapy and adds additional techniques from Behaviorism, especially the use of desensitization and conditioning techniques to help patients overcome neuroses such as phobias.

The Cognitive aspect of CBT is the aspect most heavily influenced by Stoic philosophy, but the Behaviorist aspect has proven to be very helpful for patients suffering from deep underlying fears and compulsions.

Thoughts, Emotions, and Actions

In the CBT model of how the mind works, thoughts influence emotions, and emotions influence actions or behaviors. Our actions confirm our thoughts about the world, and the cycle then repeats itself.

Attribution: Urstadt at English Wikipedia, licensed under the Creative Commons Attribution-Share Alike 3.0 Unported license.

For example, you might think that you can't relax and destress without some wine. This thought leads you to feel stressed out and tense until you do drink some wine, at which point, you feel a little bit more relaxed. The next time you have the same thought, you're more likely to act on it because your experience of drinking the wine confirmed the validity of the thought.

Of course, drinking too much wine causes other problems over time, but it's hard to break out of the loop because the connection between thought, feeling, and action seems so convincing. Even if you suspect that drinking too much is ultimately causing you much more stress, it's hard for you to accept that it won't help you right now.

At a deeper level, CBT holds that our core beliefs drive our thoughts. As in Cognitive Therapy, core beliefs are divided into three categories: beliefs about the self, beliefs about other people, and beliefs about the world.

For example, the thought that it is not possible to relax without wine might be driven by core beliefs that the world is a threatening and stressful place, that other people cannot or will not offer emotional support, and that you can't rely on anyone except yourself when you feel overwhelmed. Not knowing any other ways to relax effectively, you then convince yourself that drinking wine is the only realistic option.

This is only a simplified version of how CBT works, but the connection to Stoicism is easy to see. Epictetus would certainly agree that our core beliefs about the world inform our opinions about specific situations, generating negative emotions or paths, such as fear, and finally leading us to make unhealthy decisions. Stoicism and Cognitive Behavioral Therapy share the same basic and practical assumption that our actions are driven mostly by what we believe about the world, and the most effective way to make positive changes in our life is to change what we believe.

However, CBT does not focus on the central doctrine of Stoicism that all cognitive distortions ultimately come from the same source.

Cognitive Distortions

The main difference between the Stoic approach and the CBT approach is in the definition of what makes a thought "distorted" or unhelpful. In classical Stoicism, defining anything outside your own control as "good" or "bad" is a cognitive distortion. This is the basic error the Stoic wants to avoid. In CBT, there are four types of cognitive distortion: catastrophizing, overgeneralizing, minimizing positives, and maximizing negatives.

Catastrophizing is a type of if-then thinking in which the worst-case scenario is assumed to be true without any evidence. For example, "if I don't keep my house spotlessly clean, I'll catch a disease and die," or "if I don't get this report perfect, I'll be fired, and my career will be ruined."

Overgeneralizing is drawing a sweeping conclusion without enough evidence to support the conclusion. For example, if you go to a party, and no one talks to you, it would be an overgeneralization to assume that no one ever likes you or wants to talk to you. Your experience at a single party just isn't enough evidence for the generalization.

Minimizing positives is the habit of disregarding any evidence that things are going well for you. For instance, you might tell yourself that your new promotion doesn't matter because you'll just be overwhelmed with stress and mess things up.

Maximizing negatives is the habit of focusing too much on whatever is difficult or challenging in your life. For example, you might tell yourself you're all alone because you don't have a girlfriend, ignoring the fact that you have several close friends.

The four cognitive distortions of CBT do show some influence from Stoicism. Marcus Aurelius and Epictetus both warn us not to indulge in any "what if" thinking but to stick to the basic facts about the situation. It's not harmful to say, "my mother is sick," but it is harmful to say, "my mother is sick; what if she dies?" Avoiding "what if" thinking prevents catastrophizing.

Sticking to the facts is also a good defense against overgeneralizing. "I went to the party, and no one talked to me" is just a fact, with no value judgment attached to it. "I went to the party, and no one talked to me because no one ever wants to talk to me" is an overgeneralization. By just not adding anything to factual account, you can avoid this type of cognitive distortion.

The other two types of cognitive distortion are a bit more distant from Stoic thought because a Stoic would never admit that any external event could be positive or negative in the first place. Minimizing positives would just be "minimizing preferred indifferents," and maximizing negatives would just be "maximizing dispreferred indifferents." The Stoic way of thinking about life doesn't grant any true importance to either one.

That's the difference between Stoicism as a philosophy and CBT as a therapy. To practice Stoicism, you have to accept Stoic teachings about what really matters and what does not. Without accepting that virtue is the only good, it would be hard to practice Stoicism. To benefit from

CBT, you don't have to accept any particular belief. You just have to be willing to question your existing beliefs with the therapist's help and guidance.

Cognitive Behavioral Therapy is a practical application of Stoic insights for people who don't necessarily know anything about Stoicism.

Stages of Cognitive Behavioral Therapy

Cognitive Behavioral Therapy begins with an assessment, in which the therapist attempts to determine which critical behaviors are having an effect on the client's life. Next, the therapist decides whether these behaviors are excessive or deficient—too much or too little for the real situation. The therapist finds out how often the behavior is happening, how long it usually lasts, and how intense it is. This becomes the baseline, and the goal of the therapy is then to increase or reduce the frequency of the behavior based on the circumstances.

For example, the behavior might be excessive handwashing, a typical compulsive symptom. The therapist would find out how often the client washes his hands and how much time he spends doing so. The goal of therapy would be to reduce the frequency and duration of the behavior, so it stops causing problems in the client's life.

The next phase in CBT is reconceptualization, where the client is encouraged to think about his problem differently. This phase is similar to the Stoic approach because it's based on changing the client's beliefs about the world.

This phase is followed by skill acquisition, where the patient practices specific exercises to help him modify the behavior. Once these skills are consolidated, the therapist helps the patient generalize what he has learned in therapy. By learning how to spot the four basic cognitive distortions, the patient is given the tools to become his own therapist in the future.

That doesn't mean it's all smooth sailing from this point forward. Patients typically need some follow-up sessions to make sure they haven't slipped back into old ways of thinking.

Stoicism in Positive Psychology

Of course, Cognitive Behavioral Therapy only supports Stoicism to a limited extent because the creators of CBT didn't incorporate every aspect of Stoicism into the practical therapies they were designing. The success of CBT suggests that Stoicism is right about a few key points, especially that our happiness or unhappiness is largely determined by our beliefs.

However, CBT's effectiveness cannot be interpreted as evidence for Stoicism's most important assertions. For that, psychologists would need to test Stoicism itself, not a therapy derived from Stoicism. The purpose of therapy is to correct a disorder, but the goal of philosophy like Stoicism is to achieve well-being and happiness. This is the domain of positive psychology, a movement to redirect psychology away from the exclusive study of psychological disorders and toward the study of human well-being. Some researchers in this field have decided to test whether Stoicism can live up to its claims and improve people's lives.

In 2013, Professor Christopher Gill of the University of Exeter conducted a research study on the benefits of Stoicism with Tim LeBon of the Modern Stoicism website. The goal of the study was to determine whether Stoic training would help participants experience more life satisfaction and more positive emotions.

Participants in the study were taught the basics of Stoic practice and assigned a set of daily exercises. Exercises included a morning meditation on Stoic principles, daily study of Stoic principles and techniques, a Stoic worksheet, and evening meditation on things done well and poorly during the day. All these exercises were based on specific passages in the Stoic classics.

At the end of the week, the amount of life satisfaction reported by participants had increased by 14%. The frequency/intensity of negative emotion was down by 11%, and the frequency/intensity of positive emotion was up by 9%. Feelings of optimism were up by 18%, and 56% of participants described themselves as having behaved more ethically than usual. These are significant improvements for a study that lasted for just a single week, providing strong scientific support for Stoicism as a path toward increased well-being, happiness, and virtue.

Chapter 8:
Mind Decluttering

These days, there are so many topics that your mind can be focused on. You constantly get alerts on your phone. There's always more work to do. There are places to be, people to see, and a never-ending list of tasks to accomplish. However, it's important to learn how to focus.

This way, you will be able to place your attention on the task at hand and give your all to it. You may often find yourself caught up in what's coming next or dwelling on the past. However, you must be able to train your brain to focus on what needs your attention the most.

You must learn to declutter your mind, removing all of your unnecessary thoughts to make room for the most important thoughts. Practicing minimalism in your life can really help you to focus on what matters the most to you and what it is that you truly value in life. You must, of course, learn how to focus. There are a few ways to do this and make it easier for yourself to focus your attention properly. Finally, you can make focusing easier by prioritizing your tasks. Determine what you want to focus on, and put it in writing so that you have a visual representation of your most important tasks. By doing so, you will be able to start focusing and stop being so overwhelmed by all of your thoughts.

Decluttering Your Mind

You must declutter your mind; it is essential to your mental health, productivity, and ability to concentrate. If you have a cluttered mind, you may struggle to sleep at night. You won't be able to focus on work. It will be difficult to enjoy your life when you are weighed down with countless thoughts and filled with worries. There are a few ways that you can work on decluttering your mind.

One way to declutter your mind is to declutter your physical space. You may be mentally overwhelmed because of the physical environment that you are in. If your workspace is unorganized and filled with junk, your mind will reflect that; you won't be able to focus on your work. For this reason, it's necessary to go through your space and get rid of anything that you don't need. This will allow you to focus on what's important. Your home, workspace, and car will all influence your mental health. Put yourself in an environment that helps you to focus instead of distracting you from focusing.

Another way to declutter your mind is learning how to not multi-task. It is instinctual to multi-task, as it seems like a way of getting more done. However, you are splitting your focus among several tasks instead of giving your total focus to one. This will result in work that is of a lower quality, and you will feel overwhelmed as a result. Start making it a habit to completely finish one task before moving onto another. You will notice a dramatic change for doing so, as you will accomplish more and feel better about your work.

Be decisive. Instead of putting tasks off until later, decide what to do at the moment. If you have an important task that will take less than five minutes to accomplish, get it done first. Overthinking frequently occurs as a result of a potential decision; you don't want to make the wrong choice.

If you struggle with making a decision, jot down all of the potential pros and cons of making each choice. Use that to guide you in the decision-making process. You will receive the opportunity to make more decisions each day. If you let those collect by constantly putting them off until later, it is inevitable that you will reach a point where you feel extremely overwhelmed. Decide what to do with the tasks that matter and eliminate those that don't. For decisions you must make, get it over with instead of procrastinating.

You can also declutter the number of decisions that you must make. You may also prepare ahead of time so that you feel better when it actually happens. For instance, you may plan your outfits for the entire week on Sunday night. You may meal-prep so that you don't have to worry about food when it's mealtime.

Make a schedule for routine tasks you must complete, such as doing laundry every Thursday morning or vacuuming every Wednesday night. Reducing your decisions and coming up with a schedule can really help you to stop overthinking and have a schedule that you already know works for you. You may make a schedule for yourself so that you know exactly what to do.

Minimalism

Minimalism, typically regarded as an intense trend, is actually quite helpful for those who wish to focus more clearly. Although there are some that take this to the extreme and live out of a suitcase and choose to not have a home or car, minimalism is a practice of being more mindful of what you choose to keep in your life. It can be applied across your life to help you to only have what matters to you in your life. You may find yourself practicing minimalism in one area of your life, only to have that affect other areas of your life.

Minimalism isn't simply getting rid of things or decluttering your belongings. It is seeing what truly matters to you and sticking with that. Marie Kondo's method is to only keep items that "spark joy." This means that you only keep the items in your life that truly make you happy. It can really help you to go through each item that you own and decide what matters to you. You may have some things that you keep out of guilt or for "someday in the future." However, these items will only disappoint and frustrate you each time you see them. It is important to eliminate any items that bring you negativity or remind you of failure. Surround yourself with items that bring you joy and make you a better person. Your surroundings should be a reflection of you and what you love. You may choose to go through the items in your house, at work, in your car, and any other places that you may have. Do not bring any other items into your life that bring you down in any way; only own what you truly need to make you happy. This can help you to have a much clearer mind.

Additionally, you may practice digital minimalism. You may feel overwhelmed with the amount of information that you have coming in. There will constantly be e-mails, texts, and other notifications. Social media can also be quite overwhelming. Delete any apps that you don't use or that you don't find happiness from.

Get rid of that educational app that you "should" be using but never do. Get rid of those storage-sucking apps that you don't like. Clean up your phone. Turn off notifications that you don't need. You may go through your e-mails and delete all the ones you don't need. Unsubscribe from e-mails. Create a labeling system. For social media, unfollow those who don't have a positive effect on your life. You may even choose to stop using social media or go on a social media detox.

Limit yourself to a certain amount of time for social media. There is so much information that comes from social media, and much of it is unnecessary. Make sure that you are spending your time the way you want to be spending it.

Learning to Focus

Take some time to reflect on where you stand with your focus. Are you happy with your ability to focus? Do you wish that your focus could be improved? Figure out what your goal is. Do you find yourself getting distracted easily, unable to continue work after taking a break, or simply can't finish tasks with ease? Determine what it is that prevents you from focusing.

You may try to challenge yourself. Give yourself a task and a time limit and do your best. Become aware of how often you become distracted and how easily you can regain your focus. Write down anything that distracts you; you may not even realize how distracted you become! Afterward, ensure that you rid yourself of any distractions. Turn off your notifications. Make sure that it's quiet and peaceful. Whatever distracts you, make sure it's eliminated. You may also come up with a schedule for your breaks. Figure out what works best for you. Perhaps you like to work for fifty minutes and take a ten-minute break. Perhaps you prefer to work longer and have a longer break. It will depend on your personal preference. Regardless, it's important to remain completely focused while you are working and to also take breaks regularly. This will increase your productivity and allow you to be less stressed. Determine what sets you off. What is it that makes you lose your focus? Why do you overthink? Reflecting can really help you to determine the causes of your actions.

There are a few ways that you may work on your focus. Meditating can really help you to be calm and live in the moment. You will learn how to become a master of your mind. This can really help if you feel overwhelmed by your thoughts. Although meditation can seem difficult (and even frustrating) at first, it provides you with a great boost to your mental health, ability to concentrate, and overall emotional well-being. Another way to help you to focus is by doing some physical activity. Taking a quick walk can help to get your blood flowing, ease up tension, and wake you up. It can be quite refreshing to get moving, even if you simply take a moment to stretch. Remaining active can also help improve your physical health, which affects your mental health. This is why keeping your physical health in check is so important. Getting the proper amount of sleep, consuming the right foods, and drinking enough water every day is crucial. You will not only feel better, but you will also be able to focus much better.

Overall, it's important to take care of your mental health so that you can focus better. By taking some time to yourself and doing small things that you love, you can really help yourself to feel better. When you are happy, you will feel much more motivated and find it much easier to focus.

Prioritizing

Perhaps you are able to focus, but you simply aren't focusing on what you should. It can be quite easy to get caught up in tasks that are unimportant or aren't urgent. You may think that you're being productive, but you're really procrastinating. This is why prioritizing is so important.

You must be able to recognize where you should be placing your focus. Otherwise, it's like you're on a treadmill. You're still getting something done, but you aren't actually going anywhere. You must learn to prioritize your tasks properly so that you focus first on what's important. After that, you may move on to other tasks.

One way to prioritize is by making to-do lists every day. It is helpful to make them the night before so that you can plan ahead of time. At the moment, you may not feel as motivated to accomplish every task. It helps to have one to three major tasks for the day. These are your top tasks. Even if they are the only things you accomplish for the day, you would be happy with yourself. These are your top priority, and it is what you should focus on accomplishing first. This will allow you to focus on what you must.

You should also write down any additional goals that you have for the day. Write every possible thing that is on your mind. Make a list of all of the potential tasks, even if they aren't necessary for the day.

By doing a "brain dump," you are freeing yourself of clutter in your mind. This will really help you to focus on the present instead of the past or future. Additionally, you will feel better knowing that you won't forget anything that you would like to do. It will all be written down, so you can feel more at peace.

Brain Dump
Need to do progress towards completing a project, go grocery shopping, go to the bank, clean kitchen, take the dog to the groomer, do laundry and wash sheets, go to the gym, talk to sister about dinner, schedule dentist appointment, etc.

You may also consider journaling to help you figure out what matters. Each day, you may reflect on your day. Determine what your strengths and weaknesses for that day were. How was your focus? Did you accomplish everything? This will also help you to determine how you can improve for the next day. Although it will take time to become better at focusing, you may practice and improve your skills every day. Eventually, you will naturally prioritize your tasks and focus. Until then, you must make a conscious effort to do so.

Conclusion

Communication basically involves three things, verbal, non-verbal skills and assertiveness. Mastering these three skills will make you a better communicator. Non-verbal skills include the body language, gesturing, eye contact, smiling and the tone of the voice.

Effective conversation plays a major role in any workplace. For an institution to achieve its goals and prosper, effective communication is a compulsion. An institute whether big or small, depends on its employees. An employee can be strength of an institute if he/she has effective conversation skills otherwise it may be a cause of an institute's downfall.

Some institutions arrange different seminars and workshops where they train their employees about effective conversation skills. These trainings help the employees to express their ideas more effectively and appropriately. There are many advantages of effective conversation at a workplace. Some are as follows:

Effective conversation motivates the employees and improves their morale. Employees are able to perform capably when they are contended with their jobs. When the leader is effectively giving feedback to his/her employees and conveying all the required knowledge and information, only then it will increase the employee's motivation to perform well.

Team building is very important for the goal achievement of any company. Effective conversation helps in building teams comprising of managers and employees who trust each other. It creates an environment in which employees work together towards achieving their common goals.

It also reduces unwanted competition between employees. Furthermore, a manager who expresses his ideas effectively to his employees is able to build a positive relationship with his employees that will result in high productivity, eventually benefiting the institute/company.

Effective conversation can also help to overcome the barriers that arise due to workplace diversity. The aim of achieving common goals causes the employees to work effectively and avoid any sort of cultural and language differences through effective conversation.

CPSIA information can be obtained
at www.ICGtesting.com
Printed in the USA
BVHW090334040521
606332BV00006B/1048

9 781802 666588